Investigating Landforms

Lynn Van Gorp, M.S.

Earth and Space Science Readers:

Investigating Landforms

Publishing Credits

Editorial Director
Dona Herweck Rice

Associate Editor
Joshua BishopRoby

Editor-in-Chief
Sharon Coan, M.S.Ed.

Creative Director
Lee Aucoin

Illustration Manager
Timothy J. Bradley

Publisher
Rachelle Cracchiolo, M.S.Ed.

Science Contributor
Sally Ride Science

Science Consultants
Nancy McKeown,
Planetary Geologist
William B. Rice,
Engineering Geologist

Teacher Created Materials
5301 Oceanus Drive
Huntington Beach, CA 92649-1030
http://www.tcmpub.com

ISBN 978-0-7439-0557-2

Table of Contents

What Are Landforms?

Imagine yourself on a hike with your friends. You see the **mountains** all around you. Ahead is an outcropping of rocks. It seems like a giant hand just stuck the rocks in the side of the mountain. Just past them, you can see an open valley. It's wide and green. You sit and wonder. How did all of this come to be?

These things you see on that imaginary hike are types of **landforms**. Landforms are the features on Earth's surface. They are made through natural processes. Earth's surface is always changing. Scientists study landforms to learn about changes

of the past. In that way, perhaps they can predict future changes to the earth as well.

Two types of forces change Earth's surface. **Constructive forces** are such things as **earthquakes** and **volcanoes**. They build up the surface. **Destructive forces** wear down the surface. **Weathering** and erosion are examples of these.

Many landforms such as Bryce Canyon in Utah are famous. They provide us with beautiful scenery and opportunities for activity and adventure.

Types of Landforms

Mountains, **plains**, and **plateaus** are all types of landforms. A plain is a landform made of flat or gently rolling land with low **relief**. Relief is the difference between the highest and lowest parts of a landform. A mountain is a landform with high **elevation** and high relief. Elevation is a landform's height above sea level. A plateau is a landform that has high elevation and no **slope**. Slope is the slant of the ground surface.

Geomorphology

The study of landforms is called **geomorphology**. It is the part of earth science that studies the changes in Earth's surface. It also looks at the forces and processes that create them.

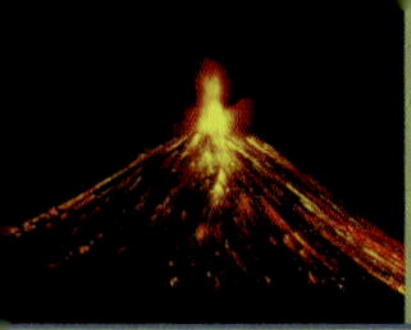

Mapping the Earth's Surface

People use maps all the time to figure out where they are going and how to get there. There are many different types of maps. Some show the surface features of an area. They are called **topographic** maps. They show elevation, relief, and slope. These maps are used for many different things. They are used to plan construction for dams, bridges, and freeways. They are also used when responding to natural disasters.

Challenge

The borders of some nations, states, and provinces follow landforms such as mountains and rivers. Look at a map of where you live. Do landforms have anything to do with its borders? What about the borders of other countries?

Get Out on the Trail

There are beautiful, ever-changing landforms all around the world. Mountain bikers can explore stunning canyons or other landforms such as high plateaus. They can ride among sand dunes or along hilltops. Millions of mountain bikers challenge their strength each year. Many bike trails were once fire or logging roads, animal paths, or hiking trails. Some people thought mountain biking could damage the land. Now, the trails are better. More trails are opening all the time. So, it's time for that thrilling ride. Get out on the trail and ride!

Have you ever tried to draw a map of your neighborhood? To do it, you'll need to look at all the streets and houses. Then you'll need to note the locations of parks, schools, and other public places. When you know where everything is, you can grab some paper and pencils and start drawing. Imagine how long that takes! Now, imagine if you tried to draw your whole city. What if you tried to draw your whole country?

For hundreds of years, mapmakers gathered information and drew maps by hand. Explorers made maps from what they saw themselves or heard from travelers. It took a long time to draw these maps. No one knew how correct they were.

Making maps has changed. One change comes from photography. Now we can take pictures of landforms from airplanes and satellites. Another change came with computers. Computers can make maps quickly. The same maps would takc someone hundreds of hours to draw by hand.

During the early 1800s, Lewis and Clark traveled the Northwest with Shoshone guides, making maps as they explored.

Before and After

The greatest change in mapmaking came in 1972. Satellites were sent into space to look at Earth's surface. They sent information back to Earth. Computers use the information to make maps quickly and accurately. The effects of storms and **earthquakes** can be seen in "before and after" pictures.

August 24, 2002
New Orleans, Louisiana

September 2, 2005
New Orleans, Louisiana

Earthquakes and Volcanoes

Earthquakes

If you live in certain parts of the world, you are very familiar with earthquakes. There's nothing quite like getting caught up in all the shaking and rolling that goes on when the earth makes a big shift. Have you ever felt an earthquake? An earthquake causes Earth's surface to move and shift. A large earthquake can change the land in seconds.

The outer shell of Earth's **crust** is not one piece. As the pieces of the crust move, stress builds between them. The rock breaks when too much stress builds in one section of the crust. This creates a **fault**. In an earthquake, there is movement at the fault line. This movement can change or create landforms.

Bryce National Park, Utah

Big Bend National Park, Texas

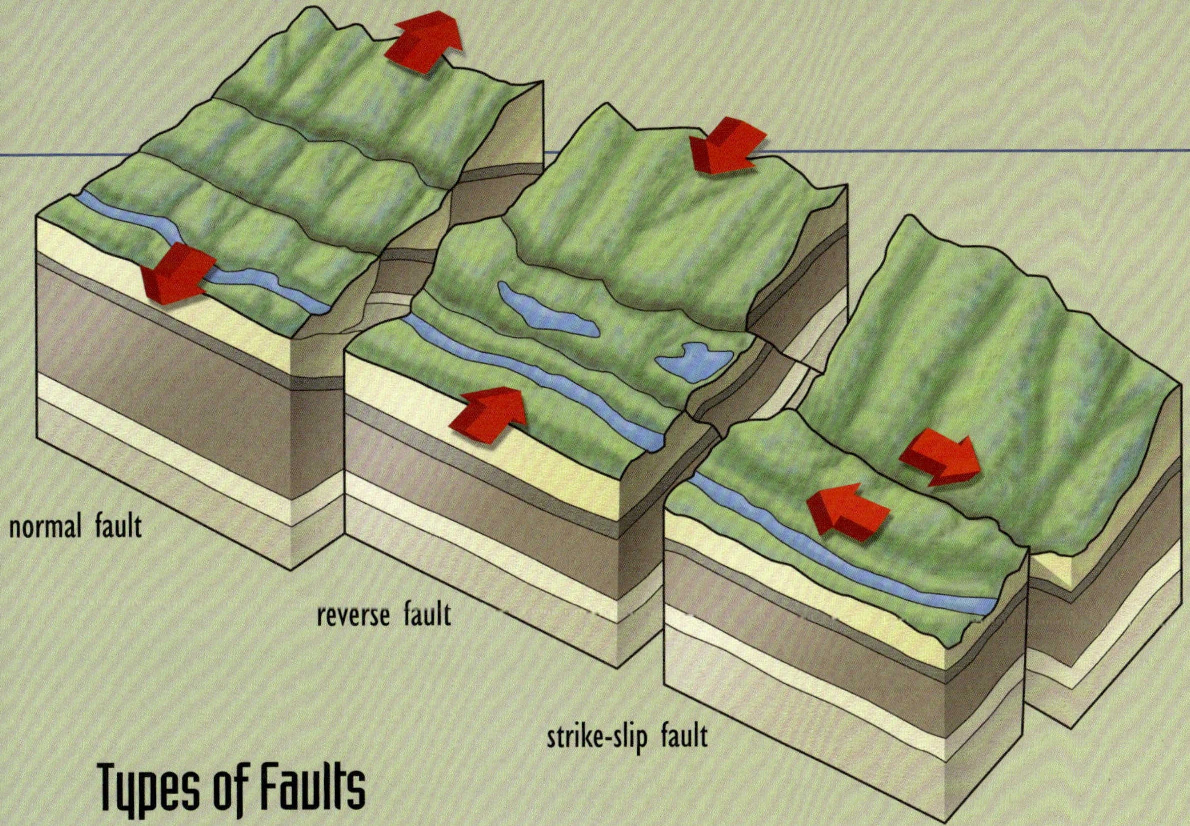

Types of Faults

There are three main types of faults. A normal fault happens when the fault line in the earth runs at an angle to the surface. The stress from an earthquake pushes out, away from the fault line. This causes one section of rock to drop below another section. The Rio Grande valley in New Mexico is an example of a normal fault.

A reverse fault also happens when the fault line is at an angle. But in this case, the stress from an earthquake pushes in toward the fault line. This causes one section of rock to move up and over another section. An example of a reverse fault can be found at Glacier National Park. (A reverse fault is also called a thrust fault.)

A strike slip fault happens when the sections of rock on each side of the fault slip past each other sideways. There is little or no up-and-down movement. San Andreas Fault in California is an example of a strike-slip fault.

Volcanoes Create Landforms

Volcanoes have made some of the most beautiful landforms on Earth. For example, Mt. Fuji in Japan and the Hawaiian Islands were made by volcanoes. Volcanoes can also cause death and destruction. Mount Etna in Italy has done just that.

One of the most recent big eruptions occurred at Mt. St. Helens in the state of Washington, U.S.A. The shape of the mountain was changed completely. Lava flowing from the volcano hardened to become new landforms.

A volcano happens when melted rock, or **magma**, inside the earth breaks through a weak spot in the crust. When the melted rock reaches the surface, it is called **lava**. Lava adds new rock to existing land. It can also form new islands.

Most volcanoes happen near the edge of the earth's **plates**. The push and pull at these borders makes the crust weak. This lets magma reach the surface.

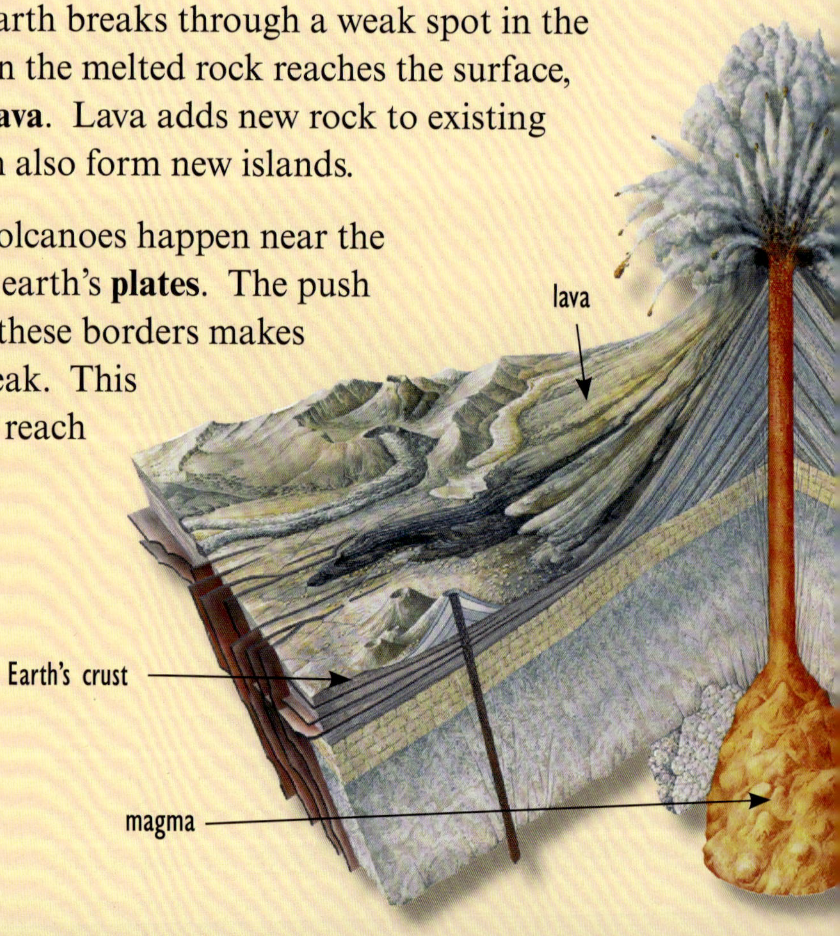

inside one type of volcano

Mountain Excitement

Have you ever thought of climbing a mountain? You don't need to start with Mt. Everest, the tallest mountain in the world. You can start with easy hikes in your local mountains. Or you can visit popular hiking and climbing spots like Lovers Leap, a granite formation in the middle of California. It has vertical cracks that are great for beginners. There are big handholds in the middle of many of the difficult climbing areas. Check it out! The perfect mountain is waiting for you. You can even climb volcanoes that are not active. Just be careful!

Fun Fact

Did you know that there are more than 600 active volcanoes on land? There are many more beneath the sea.

Types of Eruptions

Have you ever seen films of a volcano erupting? It's very dramatic on film. That's how it is in real life, too. An **eruption** happens when melted rock is forced from a volcano. There are different types of eruptions. A quiet eruption occurs if the lava is thin and flows easily. The Hawaiian Islands and Iceland were made in this way. A quiet eruption makes two types of lava. Fast-moving, hot lava hardens into a rippled surface. Cooler, slower-moving lava hardens into rough chunks.

An explosive eruption occurs if the lava is thick and sticky. It doesn't flow. Instead, it builds up in the volcano until it explodes. The explosion breaks the lava into pieces. The pieces can be as small as ash or as big as a car. Mount St. Helens in 1980 was an example of an explosive eruption.

Some volcanoes come from hot spots inside the earth. A hot spot is an area where magma melts through the crust like a blowtorch. Yellowstone National Park has examples of hot spots.

Sometimes magma can't reach the surface of Earth's crust. It hardens under the surface. It isn't seen until the rock wears away. Ship Rock in New Mexico is an example of this. Magma hardened inside the volcano. When the rock around it wore away, a huge formation remained. It looks like a giant tooth stuck in the ground.

Ship Rock, New Mexico

Mount St. Helens, Washington

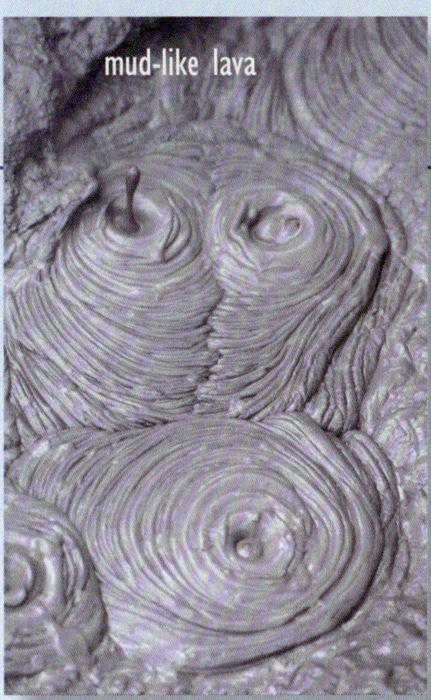

mud-like lava

The Columbia River Gorge: More Than Beautiful

The Columbia River Gorge is a spectacular river canyon in Oregon. It was created by a series of lava flows that covered thousands of square miles. If you visit, you can enjoy land activities such as hiking, mountain biking, and rock climbing. Or you can head to the water for fishing, boating, and windsurfing fun.

Weathering

Landforms change with the **weathering** of rocks and soil. Rocks are broken or worn into smaller pieces. This happens slowly. Even so, it can eventually wear down mountains.

There are two main types of weathering. They are natural and chemical. Natural weathering is done through natural processes. These processes make rock crack, crumble, and flake apart. For example, when water freezes in a crack in a rock, it expands. This widens the crack and weakens the rock. Rocks can also be worn down when ground cover is removed from the rock's surface. Then the rock is not protected. **Wind** and water often carry sand and other material across the surface of bare rock. This scratches and wears down the rock. These are all examples of natural weathering.

Chemical weathering breaks down rocks with chemical processes. Chemicals form holes and soft spots in rocks. This causes them to break apart easily. For example, carbon dioxide in

Fox Glacier, New Zealand

Running water can wash away soil, exposing roots and rocks.

water creates an acid that weakens marble and limestone. Living things such as plants make a weak acid, too. It slowly dissolves the rock around plants.

Acid rain is caused when burning coal, oil, and gas pollute our air. The pollution reacts with moisture in the air. This makes clouds filled with acids that fall as acid rain. Acid rain wears away rock.

Quick Damage

Did you know that acid rain is the worst form of chemical weathering? It causes quick changes to landforms. It also wears down buildings and statues exposed to the rain. Many ancient buildings and structures are being destroyed because of acid rain and other forms of pollution.

What Is Erosion?

Have you ever made a sand castle? What happened to it? Did the waves sweep it away? That's a form of **erosion**. There are many forces that cause erosion. The forces include **gravity**, water, **glaciers**, **waves**, and wind. Erosion is the movement of soil, mud, rock, and other particles away from an area. The materials moved are called **sediment**.

Gravity is a force that pulls sediment downhill. Landslides happen when rocks and soil move suddenly down a hillside. They create fast erosion. They often happen when part of a hillside has been cut away when roads or houses are being built.

Mudflows are the rapid movement of mud down a hillside. Mud is a mixture of rock, soil, and water. Mudflows often happen after a heavy rain in a normally dry area.

Slumps happen when rock and soil move down a slope in one large piece. Draining water creates a path under a section of rock. This water flow weakens the soil's hold on the slope. When the soil can no longer hold on, it suddenly gives way and slips down the hillside.

A mudflow has stripped away the trees on this part of the mountain.

Afraid of the Dark?

Over thousands of years, areas with limestone rocks can develop caves. One of the most exciting caves in the world is the Waitomo Glowworm Caves in New Zealand. People from all over the world visit these caves. They are an ancient maze of limestone caves and grottos. While there, you can take a boat trip through Glowworm Grotto. It is lit by millions of tiny glowworms.

Glaciers

A glacier is a large mass of ice and snow that slowly moves over land. Gravity causes the glacier to move downhill.

There are two main types of glaciers. Valley glaciers are long and narrow. They form when snow and ice build high in a mountain valley. The sides of the mountain keep the glacier from spreading out.

Continental glaciers (also called ice sheets) cover much of a continent or large island. They can flow in all directions. During a long-ago period of time called the Ice Age, they covered parts of North America, Europe, and Asia. As they moved, they changed the landscape. Today, glaciers cover Antarctica and most of Greenland.

When a glacier moves, its weight breaks apart rock. Some of the rocks are small. Some are boulders the size of houses. They freeze to the bottom of the glacier. When the glacier moves, the rocks move with it. They scratch and gouge the earth below. A glacier gathers huge amounts of rock and soil as it moves. When it melts, it deposits this material. That creates new landforms.

Have you ever visited the Great Lakes? They were formed by a glacier. A large river valley was covered by a glacier. As the glacier moved, it scraped loose sediment and soft rocks. This created large basins. The basins filled with water as the glaciers melted. The Great Lakes were born.

Hikers explore the Bugaboo Mountains in British Columbia, Canada.

Glaciers: Not Just Old Ice

Do you think climbing, hiking, and skiing on hills and mountains is a challenge? Try a glacier! The Canadian Rocky Mountains are one of the world's best mountaineering and climbing areas. You will find huge glacial areas. They make up just a small part of the thick ice mass that once covered Western Canada's mountains. You can travel out onto the ice and explore. You can just look at all the beauty around you. One thing is for sure. You have to see a glacier to really understand its size and beauty.

Running Water

Did you ever make sand castles? What happens if you pour water over a pile of sand? The pile crumbles? Running water changes more of the earth's surface than any other form of erosion. **Runoff**, streams, and rivers are all types of running water.

More runoff means more erosion. The faster the water moves, the larger the objects it can carry. Water picks up sediment. It carries it and then drops it. Trees and other ground cover slow erosion. They hold back some of the water and keep the soil and rock in place.

Floods can cause widespread property damage.

Heavy rains can cause rivers to flood. Floods cover the nearby land with water. When the water goes back, it leaves behind rich soil. This soil is perfect for growing crops.

Erosion creates waterfalls, too. Waterfalls form when water passes over hard rock. Niagara Falls was made because the top layer of rock was harder than the layer below it. The river washed away the soft rock more quickly than the layer on top. Finally, pieces of the hard top layer broke away. This caused the waterfall's sharp edge and drop.

World's Tallest Waterfall

The tallest waterfall in the world is Angel Falls in Venezuela. It is 20 times taller than Niagara Falls, which gets millions of visitors each year. Angel Falls is in the middle of a thick rain forest. There are no roads to the waterfall, so not many people get to visit.

a dust storm during the dustbowl in the 1930

Wind

You have probably tried walking on a very windy day. Sometimes it can feel as though the wind wants to blow you from side to side. Sometimes it can almost keep you from moving forward. If you're not careful, a strong wind can knock you right off your feet.

Wind can cause a lot of damage. It also causes great change in deserts. Desert land has very few plants to hold the sand in place. Wind blows over the desert, picking up the smallest things and carrying them until they fall. Fast-moving wind can carry more than slow-moving wind can. Lighter materials are carried higher and faster than heavier materials.

A sand dune can be formed when the wind hits something like a rock or a plant. It drops what it is carrying. Sand dunes can be found along beaches and in a desert. Have you ever been to a sand dune? Some people go there to ride go-carts or motorcycles.

During the 1930s in the United States, farmlands lost a lot of topsoil. Dust storms happened regularly. Part of the problem was that there were no trees on the ground to hold the soil. Farmers learned that planting trees helps hold the soil in place. Now there are more trees separating sections of farmland.

a sandstorm in the Sahara Desert

Super Sand Dunes

The Namib Desert along Africa's coast has some amazing sand dunes. They are as tall as the tallest skyscrapers and miles wide.

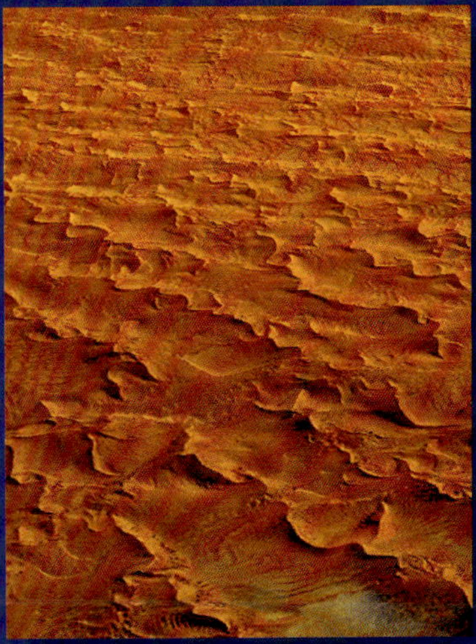

Waves

Waves are beautiful to watch, and fun to ride on a surfboard or your belly. They play a role in shaping the land, too. Waves in oceans and lakes shape beaches. They erode the shore in some places and build it up in others.

Wind is one source of energy for waves. It blows across the water's surface. This makes an up-and-down motion. When the force of a wave hits the shore, it can form cliffs and caves. It breaks rocks into small pieces. The energy of waves and the salt in the water erode the rocky coastline.

Waves can change sandy beaches that have no rock, too. Sand can be removed from a beach and taken away from the shore. Depending on the wind force and direction, it can make its way back to the shore again.

damage done by a tsunami in Indonesia

Many communities build seawalls to protect their shores from erosion. People fill sandbags and stack them along the areas most in danger. This helps keep the sand in place.

A tsunami is another source for making waves. It is an enormous wave that is caused by an underwater earthquake. Since the Indian Ocean tsunami in 2004, scientists have tried to retrace the path of those waves. They want to learn how and why the water moved in the directions it did. The more they learn, the better prepared people can be.

Underwater Diving

Landforms happen underwater, too. There are many beautiful underwater places to visit. One that can't be missed is Australia's Great Barrier Reef. It is the largest protected sea area in the world. It has almost 3,000 reefs. There are more than 600 continental islands. Swimming everywhere are thousands of fish, sea snakes, sea turtles, whales, dolphins, and porpoises. Pull out your snorkeling gear. It's time to head "down under" to the Great Barrier Reef!

Let's Experiment

Lab: Earth Movement

This lab will explore the effects of rainfall on the movement of earth down a slope.

Materials

- soil
- sand
- gravel
- large tray with edges
- water
- watering can

Procedure

1 Build a model mountain on the tray with the gravel, sand, and soil.

2 Use the watering can to sprinkle water on the mountain. What does this simulate?

3 Increase the water flow on the mountain to a pour. What does this simulate?

4 Record what you see. What type of movement took place (landslide, mudslide, or slump)? Was the movement different depending on the flow of the water? If yes, in what way?

5 What type of force is responsible for this type of movement?

Extension Idea for Further Study

- Create different landforms such as hills, valleys, and plains.
- Test the effects of different forces such as wind.

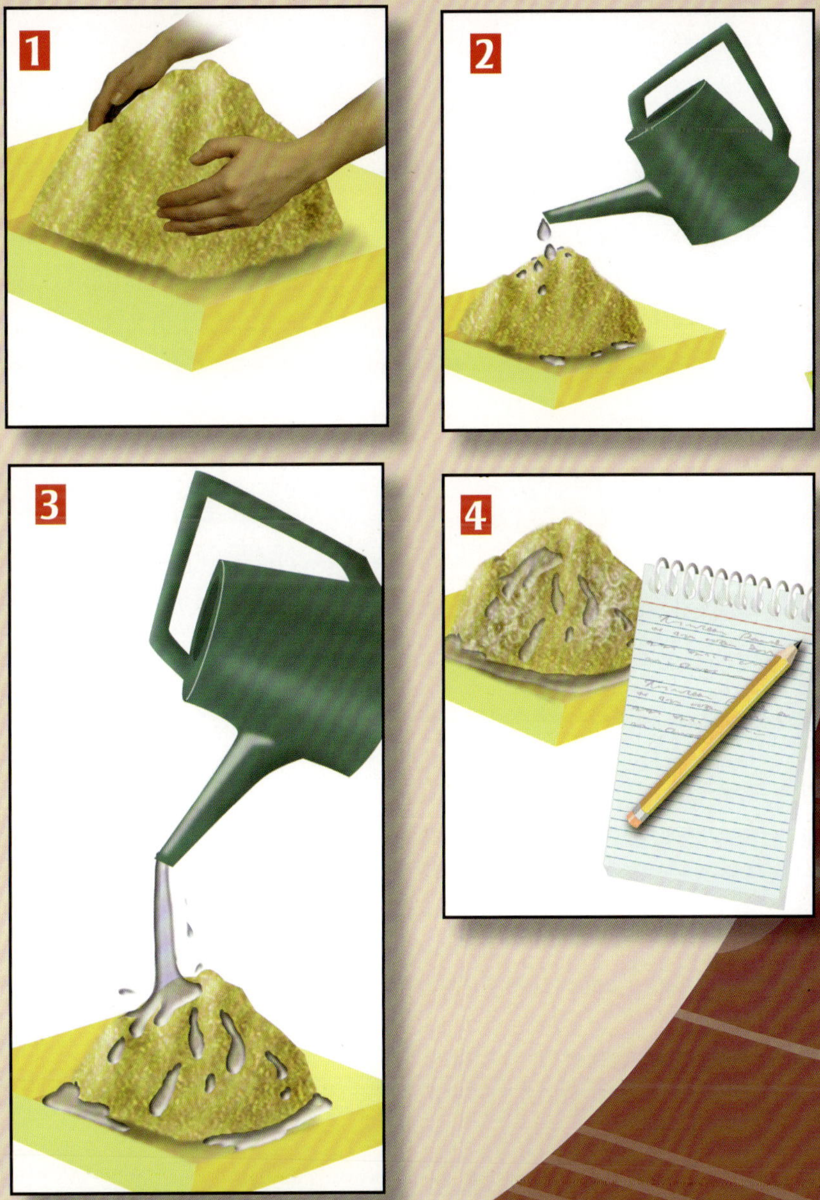

Glossary

constructive forces—forces such as earthquakes and volcanoes that build up the earth's surface

crust—the outermost layer of a planet or moon

destructive forces—forces such as weathering and erosion that wear down the earth's surface

earthquake—the shaking and trembling that causes Earth's surface and the rock beneath the surface to move

elevation—height above sea level of a landform

erosion—the movement of soil, mud, rock, and other particles away from an area

eruption—when a volcano explodes or oozes, sometimes suddenly

fault—surface trace of a break in the earth's crust

geomorphology—the study of the features and landforms of the earth and the forces and processes that create them

glacier—large mass of ice and snow that slowly moves over land

gravity—force that pulls sediment downhill as landslides and mudflows

landform—shape or form of a specific feature of the earth's surface

lava—molten rock that reaches the earth's surface, often through a volcano

magma—molten rock in the earth's crust

mountain—landform with high elevation and high relief

plain—landform made up of flat or gently rolling land with low relief

plateau—landform that has high elevation and a level surface

plates—sections of the earth's lithosphere that are constantly moving in relation to the other sections

relief—difference between the highest and lowest parts of a landform

runoff—water moving across the surface of the earth as opposed to soaking into the ground

sediment—transported sand, mud, and rock

slope—the slant of the ground surface

topographic map—a map showing the surface features of an area by displaying differences in elevation

volcano—an opening in the earth's crust through which molten lava, ash, and gases are ejected

waves—a raised line of water that moves across the surface of an area of water, especially the sea

weathering—to be weakened by weather

wind—a horizontal movement of air that moves along or parallel to the ground

Index

Sally Ride Science

Sally Ride Science™ is an innovative content company dedicated to fueling young people's interests in science. Our publications and programs provide opportunities for students and teachers to explore the captivating world of science—from astrobiology to zoology. We bring science to life and show young people that science is creative, collaborative, fascinating, and fun.

Image Credits

Cover: Jim Lopes/Shutterstock; p.3 Matej Krajcovic/Shutterstock; p.4 (top) Jim Lopes/Shutterstock; p.4–5 Luca Flor/Shutterestock; p.5 Photos.com; p.6 (top) Bychkov Kirill Alexandrovich/Shutterstock; p.6 (bottom) Tim Bradley; p.7 Zavodskov Anatoliy Nikolaevich/Shutterstock; p.8 Bettmann/CORBIS; p.9 Geoeye.com; p.10 (top) R. Hammer/Shutterstock; p.10 (left) Michael Almond/Shutterstock; p.10 (right) Francisco Romero/Shutterstock; p.11 Tim Bradley; p.12 Gary Hincks/Photo Researchers, Inc.; p.13 Craig Hansen/Shutterstock; p.15 (top, right) Photos.com; p.15 (top, wleft) LOOK Die Bildagentur der Fotografen GmbH/Alamy; p.15 (top, center) Photos.com; p.15 (background) Natalie Bratlavsky/Shutterstock; p.16 (top) Andre Klaassen/Shutterstock; p.16 (bottom) Photos.com; p.17 (top) Photos.com; p.17 (bottom) Laurence Gough/Shutterstock; p.18 (top) Francisco Romero/Shutterstock; p.18 (bottom) Tom Myers/Photo Researchers, Inc.; p.19 Corel; p.21 Nick Hanna/Alamy; p.22 (top) Bryan Busovicki/Shutterstock; p.22–23 Mark Yuill/Shutterstock; p.23 Photos.com; p.24 NRCS.gov; p.24–25 Luba V. Nel/Shutterstock; p.25 (left) Andre Klaassen/Shutterstock; p.25 (right) NASA; p.26 (top) Pete Atkinson/The Image Bank/Getty Images; p.26 (background) Todd Taulman/Shutterstock; p.26 (bottom) Norliza binti Azman/Shutterstock; p.27 Pete Atkinson/The Image Bank/Getty Images; p.28 (top) Hannamariah/Shutterstock; p.28–29 Nicoll Rager Fuller